THEN&NOW

NEW BERN

This aerial view of downtown New Bern's Neuse River waterfront highlights the many changes that have taken place since this photograph was taken in August 1955. Today, most of the homes and businesses on the south side of East Front Street are gone, replaced by an expansion of Union Point Park as well as the appearance of a luxury hotel. The Neuse River Bridge, shown at the right, is now gone, replaced in 1999 by a new high-rise bridge located further east across the Neuse. Many of the homes also shown along the 200 block of Broad Street are either gone or have been renovated into business use. New Bern's waterfront along the Trent River, at left, has changed drastically over the last 50 years as well. (Then photo courtesy of Tryon Palace Historic Sites and Gardens.)

THEN&NOW
NEW BERN

COMPILED BY VINA HUTCHINSON-FARMER

ARCADIA

Published by Arcadia Publishing,
an imprint of Tempus Publishing, Inc.
2A Cumberland Street
Charleston, SC 29401

Printed in Great Britain.

Library of Congress Catalog Card Number:2001012345

For all general information contact Arcadia Publishing at:
Telephone 843-853-2070
Fax 843-853-0044
E-Mail sales@arcadiapublishing.com

For customer service and orders:
Toll-Free 1-888-313-2665

Visit us on the internet at http://www.arcadiapublishing.com

This postcard from the 1940s highlights many important attractions of New Bern, North Carolina's second oldest city, located in the "Land of Enchanting Waters." Included is an image of Tryon Palace, which was not reconstructed until the 1950s. Other attractions depicted are Christ Episcopal Church, the John Wright Stanly house (home of the public library), and a streetscape of Middle Street, among others. (Postcard courtesy of the author's collection.)

CONTENTS

Acknowledgments   6

Introduction   7

1.   Streetscapes   9

2.   Businesses, Churches, and Other Public Buildings   25

3.   Homes Restored   55

4.   Tryon Palace Restoration   71

5.   Bibliography   95

6.   About the Author   96

ACKNOWLEDGMENTS

No undertaking such as this would be possible without the help of others. Thanks to the following people for their assistance, advice, and encouragement: Dean Knight of Tryon Palace Historic Sites and Gardens; Victor Jones of the New Bern–Craven County Public Library; Barbara Howlett of the New Bern Preservation Foundation; Judy Avery, Wanda Lingman, Karen Gardner, and Bob Murphy of the *Sun Journal*, and Jay Tervo of By the Sea Publications. I would especially like to thank my husband James and my "greatest and only" son Nick for their help in taking photographs and organizing this project. For making it possible for me to undertake endeavors such as this one, I would also like to thank my greatest (and, well, it's only fair to mention, my only) sister, Debbie Robinson.

INTRODUCTION

To really appreciate the New Bern of today, it is important to know the New Bern of yesterday. This river town maintains its heritage by standing guard over its Colonial, Georgian, Federal, Greek Revival, and Victorian architectural styles. Its citizens still maintain an attitude of friendliness and Southern gentility. New Bern was originally settled in 1710 by Swiss and German immigrants who named it after the Swiss capital of Bern. The town was officially founded by Swiss Baron Christoph deGraffenried. Just like any Swiss city, New Bern is distinguished by its red brick clock tower above City Hall. The town emblem, as in Old Bern, is a black bear, and the symbol appears frequently throughout the city. New Bern has been fought over by Native Americans, the Swiss, the British, Colonials, Yankees, and Rebels. After each skirmish, it pulled itself up by its bootstraps and plodded onward. The result is a panoply of American history along tree-lined streets, an odd mix of architectural styles that make the town quite picturesque. Historic markers point out the houses where the first elected assembly in the colonies met in defiance of the crown in 1774, where a signer of the United States constitution lived, and where George Washington slept—twice. Markers also show you the office of jurist William Gaston, the first chief justice of the state supreme court and composer of the North Carolina state song. The second-oldest city in North Carolina, New Bern is the site of many firsts. It was in New Bern that the first state printing press was set up and the first book and newspaper were published. The state's first public school opened here. The first official celebration of George Washington's birthday was held in New Bern, and it was here that the world's first practical torpedo was assembled and detonated. In the 1890s, C.D. Bradham, a New Bern pharmacist, invented Brad's Drink, now known as Pepsi-Cola. Without question, New Bern's centerpiece is Tryon Palace, the lavish Georgian brick mansion named after William Tryon, the British colonial governor who had it built in 1770. The current palace is a reproduction of the one Governor Tryon built. What you see now was built in the 1950s. It is a sumptuous showplace inside and out. Twin rows of oaks leading up to the entrance provide a stately introduction, and the scenic backdrop is the wide and lovely Trent River. The palace is where delegates gathered for the first state legislature meeting in 1777. But even before all that, before the palace, the school, and the white man's voice, this site on the Neuse and Trent Rivers captured the interest of the Tuscaroras. It is believed that the Native Americans may have had hunting camps and villages here for thousands of years. Downtown New Bern sits on a point of land at the confluence of the Neuse and Trent Rivers. Once the main hub, the downtown area fell into great disrepair in the early 1970s due to the development of shopping malls and suburban housing outside the business district. That all changed, however, when in 1979, local government gave Swiss Bear Inc., a nonprofit corporation of civic leaders, the authority and responsibility to revitalize the downtown area. Today, art galleries, specialty shops, antique stores, restaurants, and other businesses have resurrected downtown, turning it into a bustling hub of activity.

Progressive and exciting improvements are continuously underway. New Bern's downtown blocks grow more distinctive and beautiful every day as private restoration efforts return many of the building facades to their turn-of-the-last-century elegance. New Bern has three historic districts with homes, stores, and churches dating back to the early 18th century. Within easy walking distance of the waterfront are more than 150 homes and buildings listed on the National Register of Historic Places. Also nearby are several bed and breakfast inns, outstanding restaurants, banks, antiques and specialty shops, Tryon Palace, city and county government complexes, and many of the town's 2,000 crape myrtles. The crape myrtle is New Bern's official flower, and it's no wonder. On those hot summer days when you feel like drooping, the crape myrtle seems to laugh with energy as it bursts forth in a profusion of blossoms. New Bern does its gardening quietly. Led by the example of the professionally pampered Tryon Palace gardens, the town's residents have a yen to make things grow. During the spring explosion of dogwoods and azaleas, a ride through many neighborhoods can be breathtaking. Gardens, both public and private, extend throughout the city and its suburbs. In addition to the Downtown Historic District, New Bern's Ghent and Riverside neighborhoods carry official historic neighborhood designations. To really get to know New Bern, you have to take it as it is. Think of the river city as a slow treasure hunt where gems are revealed as you walk its streets. It is there that you will discover the real New Bern. Visit its museums, take time to read the historic markers, and be sure to say hello to the people in their gardens and on their porches. New Bern is a gentle place, a place where one can really enjoy the passing scene and where people know how to appreciate a pretty day. It's just that kind of town. (Courtesy of The Insiders Guide to the Central Coast and New Bern, www.insiders.com/crystalcoast.)

This pictorial history starts with a look at downtown streetscapes. While some streets have remained much the same over the years, others have changed completely, such as the 200 block of Craven Street, shown here, which has undergone a complete transformation since this picture was taken in 1908.

This comparison view of the south side of the 200 block of Pollock Street shows how, in some cases, many New Bern neighborhoods have changed very little over time. The house at the far right is the Mrs. William P.M. Bryan House, built *c.* 1926 in the Dutch Colonial variation of the Colonial Revival style popular at that time. The house to its left, the James M. Howard House, dates from *c.* 1890 and is one of New Bern's few existing examples of Queen Anne–influenced architecture. The Simpson-Oaksmith House (now gone) also can be seen in the distance. Many of downtown's historic homes now house businesses and offices, particularly in the 200 block of Pollock Street. (Then photograph courtesy of the New Bern Firemen's Museum Collection, New Bern-Craven County Photographic Archive, New Bern-Craven County Public Library.)

This *c.* 1930 postcard view of Pollock Street, looking west, includes the David F. Jarvis House, built in 1903 for "one of the leading and popular merchants of New Bern," and a brief glimpse in the distance of the steps of the U.S. Post Office, courthouse, and customs house (now New Bern City Hall). One cannot help but think the existence today of overhead power lines detracts from New Bern's otherwise charming appearance; however, a plan by the city to move these lines underground in certain downtown areas has stalled due to economic problems and a corresponding lack of funding. (Then postcard view courtesy of the author's collection.)

POLLOCK STREET, LOOKING WEST, NEW BERN, N. C. 14

With today's paved, smooth roads, one finds it difficult to imagine when New Bern streets were otherwise. This *c.* 1870–1880 view of the 700 block of Pollock Street, looking west from Eden Street, includes (to the left) the Jones House at 231 Eden Street. Built *c.* 1809 and enlarged in 1820, the house was used as a jail during the Civil War when Federal troops occupied New Bern. Currently it is home to one of Tryon Palace's gift shops. (Then photograph courtesy of the New Bern Firemen's Museum Collection, New Bern–Craven County Photographic Archive, New Bern–Craven County Public Library.)

A *c.* 1950 postcard view of Broad Street to the west shows the Mohn Building, constructed in 1927, on the right. Located on the corner of Middle and Broad Streets, it was designed to house several businesses, the most prominent one being Clark's Drug Store, which was located on the corner. During the 1980s, the building was remodeled and the storefront and windows were updated to their current appearance. It now houses offices. To the left, although partially obscured by trees in this postcard, is the *c.* 1912 Stanly Building, which housed the well-known and popular Williams Restaurant from the late 1930s to 1981. The first business to occupy the building was the Bradham Drug Co., which leased the store in 1913. This was the second location of a drug store owned by Caleb Bradham, the inventor of Pepsi-Cola. Today the Stanly Building is home of The Chelsea, a restaurant. Broad Street itself was widened in the late 1950s from two lanes to four lanes, and many of its old trees were removed at that time. (Then postcard view courtesy of the author's collection.)

Broad Street Looking West
New Bern, North Carolina

The lower end of Craven Street has changed a great deal since this *c.* 1900 photograph. Looking south from South Front Street, the area was home to warehouses, steamship company offices, and other businesses, as well as various docks along the waterfront. As New Bern's dependence on the water lessened as a result of the emergence of rail transportation, the waterfront area went into a decline. Most of the buildings along the waterfront were demolished as a part of an urban renewal project in the 1970s. In the 1980s, a luxury hotel and inn were built on the site. (Then photograph courtesy of the New Bern-Craven County Public Library Collection.)

What a difference a century makes, as shown in this view of the 300 block of Middle Street, looking north. At right is the Lady Blessington cannon, which was removed from a British ship during the Revolution and placed on the corner of Middle and Pollock Streets. The cannon served as a focal point for an 1810 survey of New Bern. The buildings on the left were replaced in just a few short years by the Elks and the Kress Buildings, among others. (Then photograph courtesy of the Miss Sadie Whitehurst Collection, New Bern–Craven County Photographic Archive, New Bern–Craven County Public Library.)

This view of the 200 block of Middle Street, looking north, dates from around 1910. Once home to dry good stores, saloons, billiard parlors, and stationers, Middle Street today houses a variety of restaurants, galleries, antique stores, and gift shops. Many of its buildings' facades have been renovated time and time again and look nothing like the original, yet they manage to retain an old-fashioned look. Middle Street and its sidewalks were renovated in the 1990s, with overhead power and telephone lines being placed underground, thus adding to this street's charm. In addition, today's visitors will note the placement of trees along the street, which add visual appeal and contribute to a better environment. (Then photograph courtesy of the New Bern Historical Society Collection, New Bern–Craven County Photographic Archive, New Bern–Craven County Public Library.)

This *c.* 1960 view of the 400 block of Middle Street looks south. At right is the Mohn Building, which housed Clark's Drug Store, among other businesses. At left can be seen the J.C. Penney Building and the steeple of Christ Episcopal Church. Today the view is almost the same, although the buildings' occupants have changed and the J.C. Penney Building is gone, replaced by an open green. Here, every December, Santa Claus hears the Christmas wish lists of the area's good little boys and girls at his Santa house. (Then postcard view courtesy of the author's collection.)

The 300 block of Middle Street has changed little over the past 80 years, as this *c.* 1920 postcard, looking south, demonstrates. Businesses in the 300 block shown on the left (and their construction dates) included The Peoples Bank (1913), the J.M. Mitchell Building (1912), the Blades Block (1908–1909, commonly known as the Kress Building after a long-time occupant), and the Elk Building (1908). On the left can be seen the ornamental cast-iron fencing, which surrounds the Christ Episcopal Church grounds and dates from 1900. While the buildings remain essentially the same, currently they house businesses such as gift shops and art galleries, while the upstairs have been renovated into apartments. The addition of old-fashioned lamp posts, colorful New Bern flags, and trees make this street one of New Bern's most picturesque. (Then photograph courtesy of the Mrs. Roger Wernicke Collection, New Bern-Craven County Photographic Archive, New Bern-Craven County Public Library.)

Another postcard view of the 300 block of Middle Street, dating from the late 1940s, shows the slight changes that took place in just 20 years or so. S.H. Kress and Co., which moved in during the 1920s, occupied the first floor of the Blades Block. The *c.* 1871 Weinstein Building, which housed the O. Marks Dry Good Store and faced Pollock Street, was replaced in 1927 by the McLellan Building, which housed McLellan's Variety Store and faced Middle Street. Across the street, the building that had housed Caleb Bradham's first drugstore, where he invented Pepsi-Cola, was replaced during the late 1930s by the Hughes Building. Then, as now, the Hughes Building offers retail space on the first floor and offices on the second. The McLellan Building now houses an antique consignment shop. The diagonal

parking now allowed on many New Bern streets, as shown below, gave way to parallel parking spaces later in the century. (Then postcard view courtesy of the author's collection.)

4—Middle Street, looking South, New Bern, N. C.

A turn-of-the-century view, looking south in the 200 block of Middle Street, depicts the condition of the streets at that time; when not dry and dusty, the streets were muddy and difficult to cross on foot. The O. Marks Building to the left, which housed a dry goods store, faced Pollock Street. It was torn down in the 1920s to make way for the McLellan Building. However, the same view today looks somewhat different from its historic counterpart. Brick sidewalks, paved streets, an abundance of trees, and the absence of overhead power lines give New Bern's Middle Street a certain charm missing 100 years ago. (Then photograph courtesy of the Miss Sadie Whitehurst Collection, New Bern-Craven County Photographic Archive, New Bern-Craven County Public Library.)

The Commission House is shown on the right in this *c.* 1900 view of George Street, looking south where it intersects with Pollock Street. The Commission House, also known as the Lehman-Duffy House, dates from around 1886 to 1888. The houses exchanged hands several times before being purchased in 1923 by local businessman Nathan Mohn, who lived there until 1973, when the house was purchased by the Tryon Palace Commission. Currently, it houses offices and meeting spaces for the historic site's staff. (Then photograph courtesy of the Amy McKnight Collection, New Bern-Craven County Photographic Archive, New Bern-Craven County Public Library.)

The intersection of Craven and Johnston Streets has changed little since this photograph was taken in 1971 as part of a state Division of Archives and History architectural survey. The prominent house located on the corner is the Jerkins-Richardson House, which was built c. 1848 by Capt. Thomas Jerkins as a rental property. By the time this photograph was taken in 1971, many of New Bern's historically significant homes and buildings were in decline or lost to demolition; the Historic New Bern Foundation was founded in 1972 to preserve New Bern's architectural heritage. The name of the foundation was changed to the New Bern Preservation Foundation in 1981. (Then photograph courtesy of the Tryon Palace Historic Sites & Gardens Collection.)

This *c.* 1910 view at the corner of Johnson and Hancock Streets, looking northwest, shows of the quiet residential neighborhood still located there today. However, the row of houses on the right is mostly gone, replaced by the New Bern–Craven County Public Library in the 1960s. (Then postcard view courtesy of the author's collection.)

Johnson St
New Bern N.C.

This view of the southwest corner of the 500 block of Pollock and Hancock Streets shows yet again how much certain streets have changed over the last 100 years. The Italianate-style home on the left was most likely demolished in the early 1930s, when the site was cleared to make way for the Blue Gable, which has become a distinctive landmark in its own right. Originally a service station for the Colonial Oil Co. of Norfolk, Virginia, it was owned by the Carolina Oil Distributing Co. from 1938 to 1981. After standing empty for some time, it was renovated and currently serves as an office building. (Then photograph courtesy of the Terry Faulkner Collection, New Bern-Craven County Photographic Archive, New Bern-Craven County Public Library.)

Chapter 2

BUSINESSES, CHURCHES, AND OTHER PUBLIC BUILDINGS

Hotel Queen Anne at Night, New Bern, N. C.

A full moon highlights this romanticized postcard view of the Hotel Queen Anne, which was located on Broad Street in downtown New Bern. In its day, the Hotel Queen Anne was one of New Bern's most elegant hotels. (Then postcard view courtesy of the author's collection.)

The Gaston Hotel is shown in this *c.* 1910 postcard view of the corner of Middle and South Front Streets. The building that housed the hotel was originally built in 1795–1800 as a combination dwelling and mercantile office. Over the years, the lower level of the building housed a number of retail establishments in addition to the hotel. Under new ownership, the Gaston Hotel was refurbished in the 1950s. Renamed the Hotel Governor Tryon, it was billed as "Historic New Bern's Showplace of the South." The building was destroyed by fire in November 1965. Many of the buildings along the riverside of South Front Street were torn down in the 1970s as part of an urban renewal effort. BB&T Bank is now located along the Gaston Hotel site on South Front Street. (Then postcard courtesy of the author's collection.)

The Hotel Governor Tryon Building was long considered a landmark in downtown New Bern. Pictured here in 1959, the hotel was destroyed by fire six years later. The week of the fire, the hotel was scheduled to host events celebrating the 20th anniversary of the Tryon Palace Commission. The events instead took place at the Sudan Shrine Temple, located at the corner of Broad and East Front Streets. The area between the Gaston Hotel and other storefronts along South Front Street had formerly housed warehouses and docks. This was filled in during the 1980s and today is home to businesses such as banks and real estate agencies, as well as the

Sheraton Grand Hotel. (Then photograph courtesy of the Tryon Palace Historic Sites and Gardens Collection.)

The Simpson–Oaksmith House (built *c.* 1843) was located on the southwest corner of Pollock and East Front Streets, and served a variety of purposes until its demolition in 1974. Our first photograph, shown above, dates from about 1884 and identified the structure's use as the "Provost Marshall's Office and Guardhouse" during the Civil War. The house was purchased by Appleton Oaksmith, who made a number of elaborate additions to the exterior by the time a broadside dated 1887 appeared advertising the Vance Academy, where the promise of "special attention given to mathematics, commercial law, book-keeping, and penmanship" was available at a cost of $55 to $75 per student for a five-month session. (Then photographs courtesy of the Tryon Palace Historic Sites and Gardens Collection.)

Appleton Oaksmith was described as an eccentric and his designs for sprucing up the home's exterior were in keeping with his personality. A visitor to New Bern in 1888 described the home, (as shown in the bottom photograph, previous page) as an "architectural curiosity" with its "blending of dormers, balconies, pinnacles, fantastic-looking tower, railings, human, griffin, and dog heads." By March 1971, when the house was once again photographed as part of a state architectural survey (bottom photograph, this page), a third floor and a two-story portico had been added to the building. Like many of New Bern's architectural treasures, the Simpson-Oaksmith House is gone, having been

torn down in 1974. The location now holds an empty lot. (Then photograph courtesy of the Tryon Palace Historic Sites & Gardens Collection.)

The Harvey Mansion, located in the 200 block of South Front Street, was built *c.* 1798 as a combination residence, warehouse, and counting room for John Harvey and remained in his descendants' hands until the 1870s. It then housed a number of establishments, including a boarding house, a military academy, and an apartment building. This view from 1910 shows the central carriageway and the "ghosts" of two entrances that flanked it. (Then photograph courtesy of the John B. Green III Collection, New Bern–Craven County Photographic Archive, New Bern–Craven County Public Library.)

From 1966 to 1972, the Harvey Mansion served as home to Craven Community College before reverting to private ownership and being used as a bed-and-breakfast inn. This picture was taken in September 1971 as part of an architectural survey conducted by the state's Division of Archives and History. At the time of this book's publication, the mansion was not in use, either as a residence or as a business. (Then photograph courtesy of the Tryon Palace Historic Sites and Gardens Collection.)

Located on East Front Street, the Thomas Sparrow House was built *c.* 1840–1842 for a prominent shipbuilder. Shown in this February 1971 photograph, it stood near the Simpson-Oaksmith House, which was demolished in 1974. This area was devastated by several fires between 1838 and 1842, and many of the older homes in this area date from that period. (Then photograph courtesy of the Tryon Palace Historic Sites and Gardens Collection.)

From 1888 to 1935, the Stephens' Brick Block served as City Hall. It was originally built *c.* 1817 as a row of four brick stores for Marcus Stephens, who lost it to the Bank of Newbern in a foreclosure. The stores were then sold to separate merchants. In 1885, one had been converted to be used as an engine house for the Atlantic Steam Fire Engine Co. By 1888, all had been purchased by the City of New Bern for use as City Hall. The building was remodeled a few years after this 1908 photograph was taken by visiting Civil War veteran William Bowden. The Craven Street building retains much of its old-style look, although its lower floors have been used by a variety of retail establishments since City Hall moved to its present location. (Then photograph courtesy of

the Francis Bowden Balma Collection, New Bern-Craven County Photographic Archive, New Bern-Craven County Public Library.)

The Gem Hotel, New Bern, N. C.

The Gem Hotel on Pollock Street, as shown in this *c.* 1915 postcard, was operated in the early 20th century by a variety of owners, the most prominent one being James Moore. He was the father of Maude Moore Latham, who later would bequeath her fortune to the Tryon Palace restoration effort. Locals say that as a young child, Maude used to take walks around the neighborhood with her father, who would tell her stories about the palace once located there. In the 1950s, the house was demolished in order to make way for an office building. (Then postcard view courtesy of the author's collection.)

The Nathan Tisdale House in the 800 block of Pollock Street stands as a good example of historic restoration, as do many of the homes along this street. Although many have been adapted to business use, they are visually much more appealing than they were back in February 1971, when this photograph of the Nathan Tisdale House was taken. The Nathan Tisdale House dates from c. 1800 and features a two-room plan and central chimney. Nathan Tisdale was a silversmith who inherited the house's lot in 1797. The home was constructed shortly thereafter for use as a residence and may have also served as his shop. (Then photograph courtesy of the Tryon Palace Historic Sites & Gardens Collection.)

Originally built in 1913 for prosperous businessman James B. Blades, this grand house was designed by the city's leading architect at that time, Herbert Woodley Simpson. The Neo-Classical Revival–style mansion was located on the south side of the 300 block of Broad Street, and was later enlarged to become the Hotel Queen Anne. This postcard view touts the hotel's location on US 17, "half way between New York and Florida" on the "Ocean Highway." The building was torn down in the 1960s, and today the site is occupied by First Citizens Bank. (Then postcard courtesy of the author's collection.)

The William Hollister House dates from *c.* 1840, although this photograph dates from an architectural survey conducted in 1971. Aside from the trees being a bit larger, the house has changed little over the last 30 years. Until recently, the home has always been occupied by Hollister descendants. (Then photograph courtesy of the Tryon Palace Historic Sites and Gardens Collection.)

Downtown Middle Street has changed subtly over the last 100 years, and even today it exudes a historic charm, as does much of downtown New Bern. The combination of different architectural styles dating from different periods of the city's history offers the casual viewer an interesting perspective on architecture in general. One can only hope that the owners of downtown business buildings will continue to restore these architectural treasures, both on the exterior and the interior. This 1908 view of the Hotel Albert on the east side of the 200 block of Middle Street was taken by Civil War veteran William Bowden during a visit to New Bern. The hotel building is still there but only its lower retail spaces are occupied. (Then photograph courtesy of the Frances Bowden Balma Collection, New Bern-Craven County Photographic Archive, New Bern-Craven County Public Library.)

On the same 1908 visit, Bowden also photographed the west side of the 200 block of Middle Street. The building closest to Bowden is now the site of the 1929 Coplon Building and next to it, the *c.* 1915 O. Marks Building. On the other side of First Baptist Church, the dry goods store was replaced in 1927 with McLellan's Variety Store Building. The Gothic Revival church building dates from 1848. President Harry S Truman attended church services here on November 7, 1948. (Then photograph courtesy of the Frances Bowden Balma Collection, New Bern–Craven County Photographic Archive, New Bern–Craven County Public Library.)

Belk's Department Store, shown in this 1940s photograph, was located downtown from 1937 until its move to Twin Rivers Mall on US 17 in 1979. It was located in the O. Marks Building and later expanded in 1964 into the neighboring Coplon Building. A false metal front was placed over both buildings to give it a sleek, "modern" look. This false metal front was removed in the 1980s and both buildings were restored to their earlier appearance as part of a downtown rehabilitation effort launched by Swiss Bear. (Then photograph courtesy of the McCotter-Raines Assoc. Collection, New Bern-Craven County Photographic Archive, New Bern-Craven County Public Library.)

Pepsi inventor and pharmacist Caleb Bradham's original drug store was decked out in patriotic bunting for the fair of 1900. Bradham invented the popular soft drink in 1898 in the basement of this building. As the Pepsi business grew, Bradham left this location, which housed a number of businesses before it was replaced around 1935 with the Hughes Building. Today, the lower level of this building houses The Birthplace of Pepsi, which contains a reproduction of Bradham's soda fountain and offers Pepsi memorabilia. (Then photograph courtesy of the New Bern Historical Society Collection, New Bern-Craven County Photographic Archive, New Bern-Craven County Public Library.)

924 Ⅳ.

The Elks Building was constructed in 1908 at the corner of Pollock and Middle Streets, and it remains New Bern's tallest commercial structure downtown. For a long time, an elk's head was prominently displayed on the corner overlooking these two streets (and can faintly be seen in this postcard) but it is now gone. The building houses retail and office space. This postcard view dates from around 1910, right after the construction of the Blades Block (the Kress Building) in 1908–1909 but before the construction of the J.M. Mitchell Building next door in 1912. (Then postcard view courtesy of the author's collection.)

The United States Post Office, courthouse, and customs house was relocated from the building on the corner of Craven and Pollock Streets to this new building on the corner of Middle and New Streets, across from Centenary Methodist Church, in 1934. Constructed from 1932 to 1934 and approved by the federal government before austerity measures were imposed due to the depressed economy, the building had a final price tag of nearly $300,000—six times the average cost of a new post office building at that time. This led comedian Will Rogers to joke that Congressman Charles Abernathy, who pushed the appropriation through Congress, not only brought home the bacon but the concrete as well. (Then postcard view courtesy of the author's collection.)

NEW U. S. POST OFFICE, NEW BERN, N. C.

6A269

ENTENARY METHODIST EPISCOPAL CHURCH SOUTH.
NEW BERN N. C

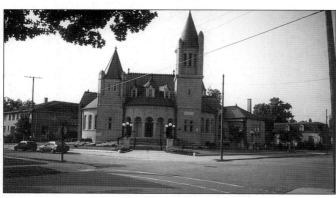

Located on the southeast corner of Middle and New Streets, Centenary Methodist Church was built in 1904. Its designers included local prominent architect Herbert Woodley Simpson. Although the interior of the church was remodeled in 1965, the exterior of the church remains much the same as it appeared in its 1905 dedication. An educational building was added to the east of the church in 1956. (Then photograph courtesy of the Mrs. Roger Wernicke Collection, New Bern-Craven County Photographic Archive, New Bern-Craven County Public Library.)

The old Centenary Methodist Church, shown here around 1901, was located on the south side of the 500 block of New Street. Located across the street from New Bern Academy, it was built in the 1840s and eventually torn down after the 1930s. The growing congregation moved in 1905 to a much larger church constructed on the corner of Middle and New Streets. The parsonage, part of which is shown to the left in this picture, still stands, although its Victorian front porch was replaced after 1931 with the present portico. (Then photograph courtesy of the Miss Sadie Whitehurst Collection, New Bern-Craven County Photographic Archive, New Bern-Craven County Public Library.)

JOHN WRIGHT STANLY HOUSE, NOW PUBLIC LIBRARY, NEW BERN, NORTH CAROLINA   N-7   BAYARD WOOTTE

The postcard above and the one on the opposite page at the bottom show the John Wright Stanly House, built *c.* 1779–1782, in the 1930s and 1940s, when it had already been moved from its original site on the corner of Middle and New Streets to around the corner on New Street. Stanly was a leading ship owner and shipper, and his wife died of yellow fever in 1789. The house stood empty for several years until the oldest Stanly son moved into the home in 1800. In 1791, George Washington spent two nights in this house, when he visited New Bern as part of his Southern Tour. He described it as "exceedingly good lodgings." The home passed through a succession of owners until it was sold and moved in 1932 to make way for the new federal building. It then served as home to the New Bern Public Library from 1935 to 1966. (Then postcard views courtesy of the author's collection.)

In 1966, the John Wright Stanly House was purchased by the Tryon Palace Commission and moved from its lot on New Street to its current location at 307 George Street. It was restored to its original appearance at the time of John Wright Stanly's residence. Pat Nixon, who was the First Lady at the time, came to New Bern for the 1971 re-opening ceremonies. Tours of Tryon Palace also include admission to the John Wright Stanly House, along with other historic buildings operated and maintained by Tryon Palace Historic Sites and Gardens. The Stanly House's former location on New Street is now a parking lot.

9—New Bern Public Library,
Historic John Wright Stanly Home
New Bern, N. C.

The Presbyterian Church at 412 New Street is New Bern's oldest church building still in use. It was built by local contractor Uriah Sandy in 1819–1822 for a congregation that had organized in 1817. It was used by the occupying Union troops during the Civil War as a hospital and look-out tower—the initials of soldiers who served duty in the belfry can still be seen today. The iron fence surrounding the courtyard dates from 1905. Only the absence of a few trees marked a change from the date of this c. 1930 postcard. (Then postcard view courtesy of the author's collection.)

The Bell Building was constructed in 1884 to house an overflow of students from the adjacent New Bern Academy Building on New Street. Both buildings remained in use as school buildings until 1972. Although its official name was New Bern Graded School, it became known as the Bell Building because of the school bell located in the cupola. After the school closed, it remained empty for 10 years before its eight classrooms were converted into four apartments for private use. (Then photograph courtesy of the Tryon Palace Historic Sites and Gardens Collection.)

New Bern High School's Griffin Building, shown in this *c.* 1940s postcard, was located next door to the Bell Building, and in its later years served as an extension of the grade school. The Griffin Building was torn down around 1980. The Coor-Cook House on Craven Street, threatened by the expansion of the Craven County jail complex, was moved to this lot in 1981 by the New Bern Preservation Foundation. (Then postcard courtesy of the author's collection.)

17—High School, New Bern, N. C.

UNION STATION, NEW BERN, N. C.

Union Station, located at 416 Queen Street, was constructed in 1910 by the Atlantic Coastline Railroad, the Norfolk and Southern Railroad, and the Atlantic and North Carolina Railroad, which provided passenger and freight services to the region. These postcard views of the station recall its heyday. The last passenger train came through the station in 1950; it has stood empty since 1989 and is now in need of renovation.

The New Bern Preservation Foundation recently unveiled and restored a 15-foot by 4-foot mural that was painted in 1939 and once hung in Union Station. The mural, which details cities, towns, and railroads along the coast, is currently in the New Bern Academy Museum, where it will stay until the station is restored. (Then postcard views courtesy of the author's collection.)

Designed by architect Herbert Woodley Simpson, the Pepsi-Cola Home Office, constructed in 1902 and shown in this 1908 view, was located at the northwest corner of Johnson and Hancock Streets. Local pharmacist Caleb Bradham, the inventor of Pepsi, lost the business to bankruptcy in 1923. The home office was connected to the building at right, which was known as Bishop's Mill and used as a coffin factory during the Civil War. Both buildings were torn down in the 1970s, and the lot remains empty today. (Then photograph courtesy of the Pepsi-Cola Bottling Company Collection, New Bern-Craven County Photographic Archive, New Bern-Craven County Public Library.)

Chapter 3

HOMES RESTORED

The New Bern Preservation Foundation was founded in 1972 as a committee of the New Bern Historical Society. The foundation, which became a separate entity from the historical society later that same year, was formed to save New Bern's historic structures, many of which were being lost to neglect and demolition. The foundation does not restore structures; instead, it purchases threatened properties (or accepts them as gifts), cleans and stabilizes them, and sells them under restrictive covenants to interested homeowners who will undertake their restoration. Dating from *c.* 1760 to 1780, the Elijah Clark House on Middle Street was purchased by the foundation in 1973 for $4,500 and sold later that year for restoration. This marked the foundation's first home purchase. (Photographs courtesy of the New Bern Preservation Foundation.)

The Cutting-Allen House dates from 1793, when James Cutting built this two-and-a-half story Georgian-to-federal style home on Broad Street. Cutting left this house in his will, probated in 1800, to his wife Lydia, who married Vine Allen in 1801. It was enlarged by a later owner to include a ballroom in 1856. The house was purchased and moved in 1980 to New Street by the New Bern Preservation Foundation to save it from demolition. Barbara Howlett, executive director of the foundation, said older homes such as this one have a distinctive charm all their own. (Photographs courtesy of the New Bern Preservation Foundation.)

The origins of this home, built around 1850 on Middle Street, are uncertain. However, some of the facts known about it include that in 1904 the house was moved one lot to the north to make way for the new Christian Science Church, and from 1912 to 1935, this building served as the home of the New Bern Library Association. Saved from demolition by the New Bern Preservation Foundation, the home was moved to its current location on Johnson Street in 1984. Howlett said that although the foundation prefers to keep buildings in their original locations, they will move homes when faced with no other choice in order to save them. (Photographs courtesy of the New Bern Preservation Foundation.)

Like many historic homes in New Bern, the Ann Green Lane House suffered from serious neglect before its restoration. Originally located on Broad Street, the home was moved in 1981 to Pollock Street. It was built *c.* 1805 for Ann Green Lane, and it was enlarged in 1868 by the Lorch family. In 1981, the New Bern Preservation Foundation was awarded a Gertrude Carraway Award of Merit for its historic preservation work by the state of North Carolina. (Photographs courtesy of the New Bern Preservation Foundation.)

Built in 1908 for local lumberman David S. Congdon, this Queen Anne and Colonial Revival home on Craven Street was enlarged around 1915 and converted into apartments. During the 1920s, it also served as a hospital. In 1986, it was restored to its original grandeur. Howlett said New Bern has been "blessed . . . to have a lot of people with vision who love old houses and are willing to do the work it takes to restore them." (Photographs courtesy of the New Bern Preservation Foundation.)

Very little is known about the early history of this early-1800s home, originally located in the 400 block of George Street. A portion of the eastern section of the home dates from 1800 to 1825, and it was enlarged to its current size around 1850. By the time it was moved to New Street in 1986, the house had been subdivided into two apartments. It has since been restored to a single-family home. (Photographs courtesy of the New Bern Preservation Foundation.)

This turn-of-the-century home on New Street was built according to a side-hall plan and was probably built as a rental property. In addition to selling homes for restoration, the foundation assists the new homeowners with obtaining state and federal tax credits, which can help offset the expense of restoration. Howlett said the ideal historic home renovator is a person who "loves old houses, has an interest in history and . . . a world of patience." (Photographs courtesy of the New Bern Preservation Foundation.)

The Gabriel Manigault Rains House, built *c.* 1810 and originally located on Johnson Street, was moved to East Front Street by the New Bern Preservation Society in 1990 and later restored. Rains was well known locally as a furniture and cabinetmaker, and he also advertised his services as an upholsterer and coffin-maker. A marker in front of the federal-period home indicates this house was the boyhood home of West Point graduates Gabriel and George Rains, who invented explosives for the Confederacy. Gabriel M. Rains sold the house in 1823 to merchant James M. Cuthbert. The home exchanged hands several times, was remodeled around 1880–1890, and was later converted into apartments before its restoration in the early 1990s. (Photographs courtesy of the New Bern Preservation Foundation.)

Restored in 1996, this *c.* 1890 house on Queen Street once served as a boarding house for railroad personnel. The foundation has concentrated on this area around the Union Station Depot for several years now, purchasing seven homes for restoration in this area in recent years, and moving another historic home to the neighborhood. In cases where a structure cannot be restored or moved, the New Bern Preservation Foundation many times has been allowed to go into a structure to remove items such as windows, mantels, doorknobs, faucet fixtures, and more. These items are then placed on salvage list and sold to other property owners seeking authentic fixtures for their restorations. Proceeds from the sale of salvage help fund other preservation projects. (Photographs courtesy of the New Bern Preservation Foundation.)

The Abbott-Rowe House on East Front Street was built *c.* 1885 as a two-story, L-plan structure for Jeremiah Abbott. The smaller Victorian porch on the front was later replaced with a wrap-around porch. Purchased in 1923 by Noah Rowe, a bookkeeper for the Blades Lumber Co., the home was enlarged and remodeled. (Photographs courtesy of the New Bern Preservation Foundation.)

The pictures on these two pages show the Abbott-Rowe House before and after its extensive exterior remodeling, which gives the home its current Colonial Revival and Bungalow appearance. According to Peter Sandbeck, the only major interior element to survive the 1923 remodeling is a staircase located in the center hall, featuring turned balusters, a mahogany handrail, and exceptional step-end brackets. (Photographs courtesy of the New Bern Preservation Foundation.)

The St. Cyprian Rectory is another project that the New Bern Preservation Foundation can point to with pride. Dating from *c.* 1880–1900, the rectory originally sat on a small triangle of land at the intersection of Johnson and Queen Streets. It stood empty for about 20 years and was donated to the foundation in the early 1990s with the stipulation that it be moved. Moving a home is very time-consuming, delicate work that involves the cooperation of homeowners in the affected neighborhoods and the city. (Photographs courtesy of the New Bern Preservation Foundation.)

The New Bern Preservation Foundation moved the rectory to a lot on East Front Street, where it was restored. Over a 30-year span, the New Bern Preservation Foundation has saved nearly 60 homes and structures and made it possible for the Ghent and Riverside neighborhoods to be officially recognized by the National Register of Historic Places. In addition to this, the foundation continues to explore the possibility of adding other New Bern neighborhoods to the register, as well as to work with the State Department of Transportation to rehabilitate a portion of Craven County's extensive brick road system, dating from the early part of the 20th century. (Photographs courtesy of the New Bern Preservation Foundation.)

The Disoway Duplex located on Johnson Street was originally constructed as a boarding house in about 1905 for Josephine Disoway. The original structure had only a one-story porch extending across the front. Between 1913 and 1924, the central porch with the lunette window on the second floor was added. Later converted into apartments, the structure was restored in the early 1990s. (Photographs courtesy of the New Bern Preservation Foundation.)

Chapter 4

TRYON
PALACE
RESTORATION

When New Bern presented a "Historical Celebration and Pageant" in June 1929, many city residents shared their hopes that Tryon Palace, which burned to the ground in February 1798, could be reconstructed where it had originally stood when it was built for royal Gov. William Tryon in the 1770s. In 1945, the state appointed members to the Tryon Palace Commission, which was authorized by the state legislature in 1953 to proceed with the work. New Bern native Maude Moore Latham established two trust funds and willed over $1 million of her money to Tryon Palace Commission, on which she served as chairman. When she died in 1951, her daughter May Gordon Kellenberger assumed her duties on the commission. This aerial view of the reconstruction site and downtown New Bern was taken in August 1954. (Then photograph courtesy of Tryon Palace Historic Sites and Gardens.

While the commission was busy acquiring lots on which stood houses and businesses, such as this Esso station (*c.* 1958) on the southeast corner of George and South Front Streets, some residents and property owners in the area launched what was ultimately an unsuccessful legal challenge to save their properties. Around 54 homes and businesses were removed from the Tryon Palace site. Today, the site of the gas station is now part of the complex's south lawn. (Then photograph courtesy of Tryon Palace Historic Sites and Gardens.)

Homes dating from the 19th and early 20th centuries, such as those depicted in this 1950 photograph (taken from the corner of George and South Front Streets, looking northwest) were either torn down or moved to other sites. In addition to removing houses from the restoration site, Highway 70 had to be re-routed and a bridge over the Trent River had to be relocated from George Street to East Front Street. All of this area today encompasses the south lawn and wilderness garden areas of the palace. (Then photograph courtesy of Tryon Palace Historic Sites and Gardens.)

As homes were being removed, including these in the 200 block of George Street, archaeological work on the site uncovered the east and west walls of the palace's original basement at a depth of about five feet, and other artifacts, including pieces of plaster moldings, marble and brass fragments, and lead from the original roof. By 1781, the palace was no longer in use as a government building. It housed a number of organizations, including the Masonic Lodge and New Bern Academy, until its destruction by fire in 1798. (Then photograph courtesy of Tryon Palace Historic Sites and Gardens.)

These houses on the north side of the 600 block of South Front Street between Eden and George Streets were removed during the reconstruction process. In 1939, architect John Hawks's original 1767 drawings of the palace were found in a descendant's papers housed at the New York Historical Society, and the final contract set of plans sent to England for crown approval were located in the British Public Records Office. These greatly aided the reconstruction efforts. (Then photograph courtesy of Tryon Palace Historic Sites and Gardens.)

The only original building of the palace left standing was the West Wing stable, which over time had been altered a great deal. By the time of the 1950s reconstruction, it was in use as an apartment building, shown on the left in this photo of the east side of the 200 block of Eden Street. When the city constructed a parking lot on Eden Street, it widened the street and planted a row of Darlington oaks, which were taken from the palace's front lawn. (Then photograph courtesy of Tryon Palace Historic Sites and Gardens.)

Businesses such as Parrott's Food Center, located on the northwest corner of George and South Front Streets, were closed or relocated due to the Tryon Palace reconstruction during the 1950s. At the time, most residents and property owners in the neighborhood quietly sold their property to the state Department of Archives and History, but a few refused to let go of their property without a fight, which slowed progress on the palace gardens. The courts ultimately ruled in favor of the Tryon Palace Commission in 1957, and the area was cleared. (Then photograph courtesy of Tryon Palace Historic Sites and Gardens.)

This is another 1950s view of the South Front Street side of Parrott's Food Center. During the 1950s, neighborhood grocery stores such as this were common in New Bern. When houses and businesses along George and South Front Streets were removed to make way for the south lawn and wilderness gardens, the level of the lawn was raised several feet (in Governor Tryon's day, the lawn would have sloped down toward the river) and a loop drive was built around the Trent River waterfront. (Then photograph courtesy of Tryon Palace Historic Sites and Gardens.)

The West Wing stable was the only original part of the palace complex left standing. Underneath a stucco exterior, which had to be carefully chipped away, approximately 75 percent of the stable's original brickwork remained. Its restoration was completed by the time the photograph below was taken in August 1955. The building over the years had been used for a variety of functions, including a school and church, before being converted into residential apartments. (Then photograph courtesy of Tryon Palace Historic Sites and Gardens.)

These businesses along the Trent River waterfront were removed to make way for the palace's south lawn. Governor Tryon moved into the palace in mid-1770 and held an assembly meeting in the palace's council room that December. He left in mid-1771 for a similar post and his successor only lived there for four years before New Bern lost its status as North Carolina's capital. By the time of President George Washington's visit in 1791, the palace was empty. Local residents did, however, stage an elegant ball in the palace in honor of Washington's visit. Today, the south lawn is the site of historic re-enactments (including living history camps with the Loyalist Highlander regiment, whose drummer is depicted on the opposite page) and concerts by the North Carolina

Symphony and other musical groups. (Then photograph courtesy of Tryon Palace Historic Sites and Gardens.)

The city of New Bern authorized the closing of the portion of George Street adjacent to the palace property in November 1952. In this undated photograph, the reconstructed East Wing kitchen can be seen to the right. The architectural firm of Perry, Shaw, and Hepburn, noted for other historic restorations, was selected for the Tryon Palace project. First, the West Wing stable was renovated to its earlier appearance and the East Wing kitchen was reconstructed. Finally, work on the palace itself began after extensive archaeological survey of the area was completed. (Then photograph courtesy of Tryon Palace Historic Sites and Gardens.)

An archaeological investigation in 1952 at the site uncovered the original 18th-century foundation and basement walls of the palace. This was used in the reconstruction and can still be seen during tours of the palace. Also found during the excavation were the foundation of the East Wing kitchen and the remains of the colonnades and the courtyard fence. The Tryon Palace complex, which includes a number of other historically significant buildings, and its gardens are one of North Carolina's most popular tourist attractions. (Then photograph courtesy of Tryon Palace Historic Sites and Gardens.)

As other buildings in the neighborhood continued to be removed, the palace, shown here in November 1955, was indeed rising "like the regenerated phoenix from the fury of the flame." The reconstruction involved not only the palace itself but also the curved colonnades that connected the stable and kitchen wings to the main house. At the same time, commission members were busy acquiring antiques and furnishings for the interior. They were aided by an inventory of Tryon's property, filed after a fire destroyed the New York governor's residence in 1773. Mrs. Latham also left her collection of valuable English antiques to the commission. (Then photograph courtesy of Tryon Palace Historic Sites and Gardens.)

This August 1956 view shows the guard stands and courtyard gate under construction. After the palace was destroyed by fire in 1798, the state general assembly extended George Street to the river and divided the property into lots, authorizing their sale. Houses such as these shown on the left were then constructed and all traces of the palace were eventually erased from the neighborhood. (Then photograph courtesy of Tryon Palace Historic Sites and Gardens.)

Even as work continued to remove from the site houses such as the one in this 1958 picture, restoration continued on the palace and its grounds. The East Wing kitchen is shown to the right. Today, this area includes the Blacksmith's Shop, where visitors can watch the palace blacksmith hard at work creating one-of-a-kind pieces. (Then photograph courtesy of Tryon Palace Historic Sites and Gardens.)

Houses were also removed along the west side of Metcalf Street to accommodate a brick wall that partially extends around the site. In addition to the palace and its outbuildings, the historic site boasts a number of beautiful gardens, including one that is a memorial to Maude Moore Latham, whose gifts made the reconstruction possible. Tryon Palace Historic Sites and Gardens does not just encompass the area's rich colonial history; other buildings in the complex highlight various periods in New Bern and North Carolina history. (Then photograph courtesy of Tryon Palace Historic Sites and Gardens.)

As the reconstructed palace neared completion in 1959, King George III's royal coat-of-arms once more rose in New Bern. Features on the coat-of-arms include the shield of the House of Hanover, topped with a crown jewel and flanked by a gold lion and a silver unicorn. Added touches include the white and red rose of England, purple thistle of Scotland, green shamrock of Ireland, and the fleur-de-lis of France. The mottoes on the coat-of-arms are "Honi Soit qui mal y pense" ("Shame be to him who evil thinks") and "Dieu et mon droit" ("God and my right"). (Then photograph courtesy of Tryon Palace Historic Sites and Gardens.)

A Shell gas station on the corner of Pollock and George Streets was renovated to serve as a visitor's center for Tryon Palace Historic Sites and Gardens. Visitors to the site can purchase tour tickets here, watch an orientation video about the palace, and enjoy special programs in an adjacent auditorium. Today the palace hosts a number of special events designed not only to highlight history but also to allow visitors to participate in it. A tour of Tryon Palace Historic Sites and Gardens currently includes seven buildings and 14 acres of gardens. (Then photograph courtesy of Tryon Palace Historic Sites and Gardens.)

This is the George Street side of the Shell station, which was renovated to serve as the palace visitor's center. The station offers an example of how older buildings can be renovated to serve new purposes. Many historic homes in New Bern have been renovated to serve as offices. (Then photograph courtesy of Tryon Palace Historic Sites and Gardens.)

The original plans for the Tryon Palace gardens were not located until 1992. The gardens for the 1950s reconstruction, left, were designed by Morley Jeffers Williams to reflect typical English gardens of the 1770s. Even today the gardens at Tryon Palace provide a shady and quiet respite for visitors. In addition to its many historical events, the Tryon Palace staff also hosts gardening programs throughout the year and opens the gardens to the public free of charge for special events. (Then photograph courtesy of Tryon Palace Historic Sites and Gardens.)

Barbour Boat Works was located on the Trent River waterfront from 1932 until 1997. Known for its small wooden boats, the company expanded during the 1940s to enter military production, constructing mine sweepers and destroyers. After the war, in addition to fishing vessels, Barbour Boat Works produced watercraft such as ferries, tugboats, and barges. This picture dates before the removal of the Trent River bridge in the 1950s. The site has been cleared; plans call for it to house an education and living history center for Tryon Palace Historic Sites and Gardens. (Then photograph courtesy of the Ida Harrison Collection, New Bern-Craven County Photographic Archive, New Bern-Craven County Library.)

BIBLIOGRAPHY

Barnett, Colin. *The Impact of Historic Preservation on New Bern, North Carolina*. Winston-Salem, NC: Bandit Books, 1993.

Green, John B., III. *A New Bern Album*. New Bern, NC: Tryon Palace Commission, 1985.

Hutchinson-Farmer, Vina. "Preserving Our Heritage." *Sun Journal*, March 2, 2002, p. D1.

Hutchinson, Vina. *Images of America: New Bern*. Charleston, SC: Arcadia Publishing, 2000.

Journal of New Bern Historical Society. Various issues, May 1988-present.

Sandbeck, Peter. *The Historic Architecture of New Bern and Craven County*. New Bern, NC: Tryon Palace Commission, 1988.

"Time Capsule: 1900-1999," *Sun Journal*, Jan. 1, 2000.

Young, Joanne and Taylor Lewis. A Tryon Treasury. New Bern, N.C.: Tryon Palace Commission, revised 1992.

ABOUT THE AUTHOR

A native of Kentucky raised in West Virginia, author Vina Hutchinson-Farmer graduated from Marshall University (home of the Thundering Herd) in 1988 with degrees in American history and news-editorial journalism. After graduating from college, Vina moved to Elizabeth City, North Carolina, to work for the local newspaper. Working her way south along the Carolina coast over the years, Hutchinson-Farmer has worked in writing and editorial positions for publications including *Coaster Magazine*, *New Bern Magazine*, *Tideland News* and *The Island Review*. In addition to her work as the advertorial supervisor/special sections editor for the *Sun Journal* in New Bern, she is a co-author of *The Insiders' Guide to the Central Coast and New Bern* and author of *Images of America: New Bern*, which was honored with a Willie Parker Peace Book Award by the North Carolina Society of Historians in 2001. In her free time, Vina enjoys spending time with her husband James and son Nick and exploring museums, historic sites, beaches, and parks. While her hobbies are many, Vina mainly enjoys genealogy and reading.